Dissertation

a long piece of writing on a particular subject, especially one written for a university degree

'Love that
journey for me'

- Alexis Rose

If found

Please contact
Name: ....
Phone: ....
Email: ....

Contents

Basics

Working title:

Key question:

Theme:

Supervisor(s):

Basics

Abstract:

Basics

Notes:

Key Dates

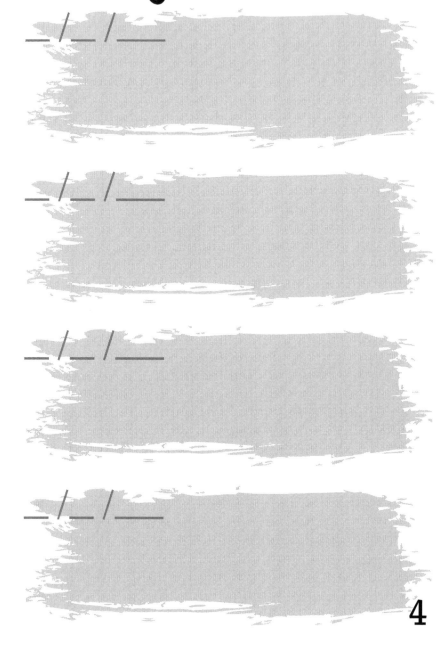

___ / ___ / ___

___ / ___ / ___

___ / ___ / ___

___ / ___ / ___

Key Dates

___ /___ /___

___ /___ /___

___ /___ /___

___ /___ /___

Key Dates

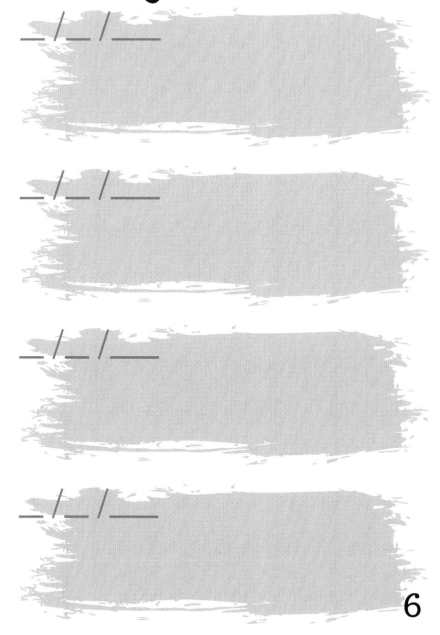

___ / ___ / _____

___ / ___ / _____

___ / ___ / _____

___ / ___ / _____

Contacts

Name:
Phone:
Email:

Name:
Phone:
Email:

Name:
Phone:
Email:

Name:
Phone:
Email:

Contacts

Name:

Phone:

Email:

Name:

Phone:

Email:

Name:

Phone:

Email:

Name:

Phone:

Email:

Overview

Introduction:

Summarise your introduction

Overview

Chapter one:

Summarise your first chapter

Overview

Chapter two:

Summarise your second chapter

Overview

Chapter three:

Summarise your third chapter

Overview

Conclusion:

Summarise your conclusion

Questions

Main question:

Other questions:

Questions

Other questions:

Introduction

Main point:

Other points:

Introduction

Key sources:

Other notes:

Chapter one

Main point:

Other points:

Chapter one

Key sources:

Other sources:

Chapter one

Notes:

Chapter two

Main point:

Other points:

Chapter two

Key sources:

Other sources:

Chapter two

Notes:

Chapter three

Main point:

Other points:

Chapter three

Key sources:

Other sources:

Chapter three

Notes:

Conclusion

Main point:

Other points:

Conclusion

Key sources:

Other notes:

Reading log

Title: ....

Author: ....

Date published: ....

Notes:

Reading log

Title: ....

Author: ....

Date published: ....

Notes:

Reading log

Title: ....

Author: ....

Date published: ....

Notes:

Reading log

Title: ....

Author: ....

Date published: ....

Notes:

Reading log

Title: ....

Author: ....

Date published: ....

Notes:

Reading log

Title: ....

Author: ....

Date published: ....

Notes:

Title: ....

Author: ....

Date published: ....

Notes:

Reading log

Title: ....

Author: ....

Date published: ....

Notes:

Title: ....

Author: ....

Date published: ....

Notes:

Reading log

Title: ....

Author: ....

Date published: ....

Notes:

Title: ....

Author: ....

Date published: ....

Notes:

Reading log

Title: ....

Author: ....

Date published: ....

Notes:

Title: ....

Author: ....

Date published: ....

Notes:

Reading log

Title: ....

Author: ....

Date published: ....

Notes:

Title: ....

Author: ....

Date published: ....

Notes:

Reading log

Title: ....

Author: ....

Date published: ....

Notes:

Title: ....

Author: ....

Date published: ....

Notes:

Reading log

Title: ....
Author: ....
Date published: ....

Notes:

Title: ....
Author: ....
Date published: ....

Notes:

Reading log

Title: ....

Author: ....

Date published: ....

Notes:

Title: ....

Author: ....

Date published: ....

Notes:

Reading log

Title: ....

Author: ....

Date published: ....

Notes:

Title: ....

Author: ....

Date published: ....

Notes:

Reading log

Title: ....

Author: ....

Date published: ....

Notes:

Title: ....

Author: ....

Date published: ....

Notes:

Monthly goals

September:

October:

November:

December:

Monthly goals

January:

February:

March:

April

Monthly goals

May:

June:

July:

August

Notes

Notes

Notes

Notes

Notes

Notes

Notes

Notes

Notes

Notes

Notes

Notes

Notes

Notes

Notes

Notes

Notes

Notes

Notes

Notes

Notes

Notes

Notes

Notes

Notes

Notes

Notes

Notes

Notes

Notes

Notes

Notes

Notes

Notes

Notes

Notes

Notes

Notes

Notes

Notes

Notes

Notes

Notes

Notes

Notes

Notes

Notes

Printed in Great Britain
by Amazon

11117329R00059